SPORTS STARS

TROY AIKMAN

ALL-AMERICAN QUARTERBACK

By R. Conrad Stein

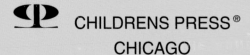 **CHILDRENS PRESS®**

CHICAGO

RR

Photo Credits

Cover, 5, ©Rob Tringoli/SportsChrome East/West; 6, ©Al Kooistra/ SportsChrome East/West; 8, Reuters/Bettmann; 9, ©Victor Baldizon/ SportsChrome East/West; 13, ©Mitchell B. Reibel/Sports Photo Masters, Inc.; 14, AP/Wide World; 16, Courtesy University of Oklahoma Sports Information; 17, 19, AP/Wide World; 20, UPI/Bettmann; 21, 22, Reuters/Bettmann; 23, UPI/Bettmann; 24, 26, 28, Reuters/Bettmann; 29, ©L. Casey/Sports Photo Masters, Inc.; 31 (top), AP/Wide World; 31 (bottom), 32, 35, Reuters/Bettmann; 36, 39, AP/Wide World; 40, ©Dave Black/Sports Photo Masters, Inc.; 43, Reuters/Bettmann; 44 (left), Courtesy University of Oklahoma Sports Information; 44 (right), AP/Wide World; 45 (left), UPI/Bettmann; 45 (right), Reuters/Bettmann; 46, ©Don Smith/Sports Photo Masters, Inc.; 47, ©Mitchell B. Reibel/Sports Photo Masters, Inc.

Editorial Staff

Project Editor: Mark Friedman
Design: Herman Adler Design Group
Photo Editor: Jan Izzo

Library of Congress Cataloging-in-Publication Data

Stein, R. Conrad.
    Troy Aikman : all-American quarterback / by R. Conrad Stein.
      p. cm. – (Sports stars)
    Summary: Demonstrates the competitive spirit of this Superbowl-winning quarterback during his years as a high school football hero, a college superstar, and a pro with the Dallas Cowboys.
    ISBN 0-516-04394-3
    1. Aikman, Troy, 1966– —Juvenile literature. 2. Football players—United States—Biography—Juvenile literature.
3. Aikman, Troy, 1966– . [1. Football players.] I. Title. II. Series.
GV939.A46S74   1995
796.332'092–dc20   95-2496
[B]   CIP
                                       AC

TROY AIKMAN
ALL-AMERICAN QUARTERBACK

On a hot, steamy night in August 1994, the Dallas Cowboys played a pre-season exhibition game against the Los Angeles Raiders. In the first quarter, Dallas quarterback Troy Aikman led his team on a 65-yard march. The drive was a stunning example of Aikman as a field general. He threw short. He threw long. He mixed running plays with passes. He confounded defenders by looking one way and throwing another. He was in complete command of the game.

At the Los Angeles six-yard line, Aikman dropped back to pass. Darting his head left and right, he saw no open receivers. So he tucked the ball under his arm and ran. At the goal line, a huge Raiders linebacker collided into him with the power of a speeding truck. The vicious tackle silenced the 60,000 Cowboy fans in Texas Stadium. Aikman had scored a touchdown, but now he lay on the ground, dazed.

Troy Aikman has no fear of running the football, which places him at risk of injury in every game.

Slowly, painfully, Aikman got to his feet. Did his fellow Cowboys congratulate him for his touchdown? No! They were enraged that he had risked his safety by running the ball during a meaningless exhibition game. Wide receiver Michael Irvin was seen screaming at his quarterback. Irvin said later, "I know what it's like without Troy, and I don't want to go into the season without him."

Dallas coach Barry Switzer said, "It's scary when Troy runs, but that's the kind of competitor he is."

He has always been that kind of a competitor, a gifted athlete who can't stand to lose.

--- ★ ★ ★ ---

Troy displayed his competitive fire even when he was a baby. He was born on November 21, 1966, the youngest of Ken and Charlyn Aikman's three children. At birth, both of his feet were oddly twisted, and his doctors wondered if he would ever walk normally. Until he was fourteen months old, he wore heavy braces, which began at the bottoms of his feet and stretched up to his knees.

When Troy was a toddler, he wore orthopedic shoes. The shoes looked like they were reversed and on the wrong feet. Despite the clumsy shoes, he scampered over the lawn of the Aikman home with the energy of any healthy three-year-old. His father and mother knew even then that Troy was special. They knew he was a competitor.

Troy grew up in Cerritos, California, a suburb of Los Angeles. He began playing sports when he was seven years old. It wasn't long before he proved himself the best athlete his age in town.

Once, Troy's fierce desire to win a Little League baseball game got him into serious trouble. "I was playing shortstop," Troy remembered, "and our coach called time out and put another kid in at second base. I started screaming that this kid was no good and shouldn't be in the game." Watching this outburst from the stands was Troy's mother. When the game ended, she marched out on the field. "My mom really chewed me out," said Troy. "She told me how embarrassed she was that I should [behave] so ugly."

When Troy was 12 years old, he and his family moved to Oklahoma to operate a farm. It was a bold decision on the part of his parents, because neither of them were experienced farmers. They settled onto a 172-acre ranch near Henryetta, Oklahoma. They raised cattle, pigs, and chickens. "That is, until the pigs ate the chickens," Troy's mother said with a laugh. "We were city farmers."

For young Troy, the move seemed to be a
disaster. He loved hanging out at the beach in
southern California. In his new surroundings,
all he saw were dusty farms. He remembers
thinking, "Man, where's the beach?"

Troy's high-school coaches welcomed the
gifted athlete. Troy played baseball, football,
basketball, and he ran track. Late in his high-
school career, he concentrated on football.

In rural Oklahoma, people follow high-school
football with intensity. Neighboring high schools
engage in football games as if they are battles
in war.

Troy's school had an odd nickname: the
Fighting Hens. To make fun of that nickname,
opposing fans used to throw rubber chickens
onto the field. In his junior year, quarterback
Troy Aikman led the Fighting Hens to the state
playoffs. "The whole town was ecstatic," said Troy.
But the next year the team suffered through a
mediocre season, and angry townspeople
responded by getting the coach fired.

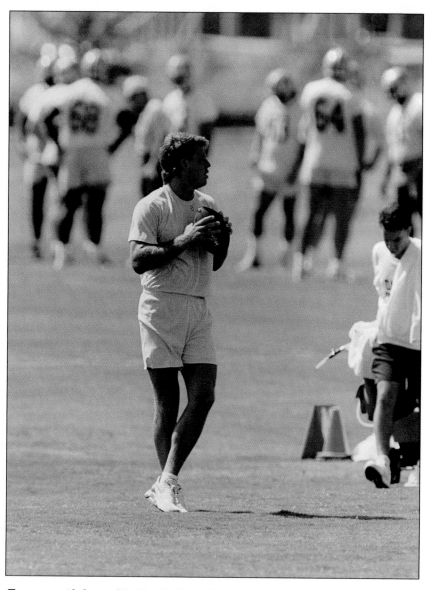

Troy practicing with the Dallas Cowboys

Even in high school, Troy displayed a magnificent quarterback arm. Throwing 40-yard passes with amazing accuracy, he thrilled the Oklahoma fans. He could "thread the needle" to zip the ball between defenders with deadly speed. He lofted rainbow passes over the defenders into friendly receivers' hands.

While developing into a high-school star, Troy grew to love his new home in Oklahoma. He still lives there. Country music is now his passion, and Hank Williams, Jr., is his favorite singer. After he became a national star, newspaper writers tried to portray Troy as a true cowboy. But is this image correct? "Heck," he said. "I can't even ride a horse."

After graduating from high school, many college football coaches tried to recruit Troy. He chose to stay near home. He accepted a football scholarship at the University of Oklahoma. The Oklahoma Sooners'

head coach was a tough taskmaster named Barry Switzer. Switzer was dedicated to moving the ball through running plays. In Switzer's scheme, Aikman could not display his strong arm and other skills at quarterback. So after two years, Troy decided to leave Oklahoma. He transferred to the University of California at Los Angeles (UCLA). The change meant the California boy was coming home. At UCLA, Troy Aikman became a college superstar.

Standing 6-foot-3 and weighing 215 pounds, Troy was big for a quarterback. Strong and swift, he ran and broke tackles when he needed to get out of a jam. Or, when pressured by enemy linemen, he threw the ball in the blink of an eye. Most important, his passes sliced through the air with speed and precision, as if they were guided missiles.

Troy in his UCLA days

In 1987, his first full year at UCLA, Troy piled up impressive numbers: 2,527 yards passing and 17 touchdown passes. The next year, he threw for 24 touchdowns. His games against UCLA's traditional rival, the University of Southern California (USC), are contests that local people still talk about years later. Troy linked up in several classic duels with the outstanding USC quarterback, Rodney Peete. (Oddly enough, Peete later became Troy's backup on the Dallas Cowboys.)

In 1989, Troy's college playing days came to an end. He was such a hot prospect that he was the first player chosen in the NFL draft. Being the number-one pick confirmed what UCLA fans already knew: Troy Aikman was the best amateur football player in the nation. Now he would become a pro and play for the Dallas Cowboys.

Dallas. The Cowboys. America's Team.

Americans love a winner, and for that reason the Cowboys have been labeled "America's Team." No other franchise has had such a brilliant record of success. During the 1970s, Dallas appeared in five Super Bowls. In that era, its roster read like a roll call from the Hall of Fame: running backs Tony Dorsett and Calvin Hill, quarterback Roger Staubach, defensive linemen Randy White and Ed "Too Tall" Jones.

When Troy Aikman joined America's Team, however, the team's glory days were a distant memory. The last half of the 1980s was a grim period for Dallas. In 1988, the team finished with a dismal 3-13 record. The franchise was in turmoil. Troy Aikman landed in the middle of this ugly situation.

Troy was drafted by the Dallas Cowboys in 1989 (opposite page). He played well as a rookie, but the Cowboys did not, compiling an NFL-worst 1-15 record.

With a new coach (Jimmy Johnson, left) and a new quarterback (Troy, right), happy days would soon return for the Cowboys.

Jimmy Johnson, the Cowboys' new head coach, boldly announced he would start his rookie quarterback and build a winning team around him. Aikman played his first game against the New Orleans Saints. The Cowboys lost 28-0. During the defeat, Troy looked confused. He was so badly beaten up that he said, "It felt like 65-0."

The season didn't get any better. Dallas finished with a pathetic 1-15 record in 1989-90. The team lost all eleven games Troy started. About his rookie year Aikman said, "There was nothing fun about football. It was time for a gut check."

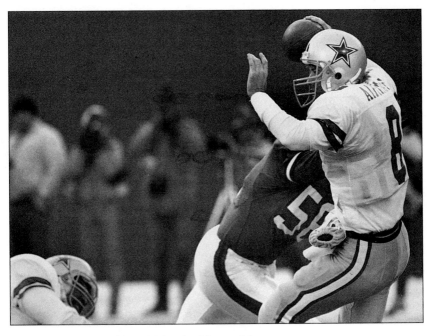

Troy took a lot of hard hits in his rookie season.

**The Cowboys became dangerous when Troy's passing was
complemented by the fantastic rushing of Emmitt Smith (right).**

Led by Aikman and Coach Johnson, the Cowboys' fortunes began to change. Other young players began to mature into stars. The speedy and muscular pass receiver Michael Irvin quickly became an All-Pro. In 1990, the Cowboys drafted the powerful running back Emmitt Smith from the University of Florida. The team's offensive game plan became simple, yet brutally effective: hand the ball to Emmitt, or throw it to Michael. This offense, combined with a swarming defense, produced a strong team in Dallas.

A turning point came in Troy's second year, when the Cowboys beat the Rams 24-21 and went on to win four straight games. They finished that season with a 7-9 record and barely missed the playoffs. The next year saw Dallas drive to an excellent 11-5 finish, and they advanced to the second round in post-season competition.

Troy reads the field, looking for an open man.

★ ★ ★

A key reason behind the club's quick success was the leadership of Troy Aikman. As a rookie, Troy rarely said a critical word to a teammate. But the Cowboys were a young squad, and somebody had to correct mistakes. "I've never minded physical errors, like someone dropping the ball," Aikman said. "But the mental mistakes, like not knowing assignments, I don't tolerate that." Dallas players learned that if they suffered a lack of concentration and made a dreaded mental mistake, they risked getting chewed out by their quarterback. As a result, Aikman gained complete control over the offensive team. The Cowboy offense played exactly as Troy always had: with intensity.

"Nobody but Troy ever says anything in the huddle," said veteran safety Bill Bates. "If he can get that kind of respect from Michael Irvin and Emmitt Smith, you know right away it's his team."

With talented players and leadership provided
by Aikman, the Cowboys enjoyed a dizzying string
of successes. In 1992-93, Dallas steamrolled over
opponents to run up a 13-3 record. They then
breezed through the playoffs and walloped Buffalo
52-17 in Super Bowl XXVII. Troy was named
Most Valuable Player of the big game for his near-
perfect performance: 273 yards passing and four
touchdown throws. After the victory, he raced
off the field shouting the traditional words of
a winner, "I'm going to Disneyland!"

**NFL commissioner Paul Tagliabue (right) presents Troy with
the 1993 Super Bowl MVP trophy.**

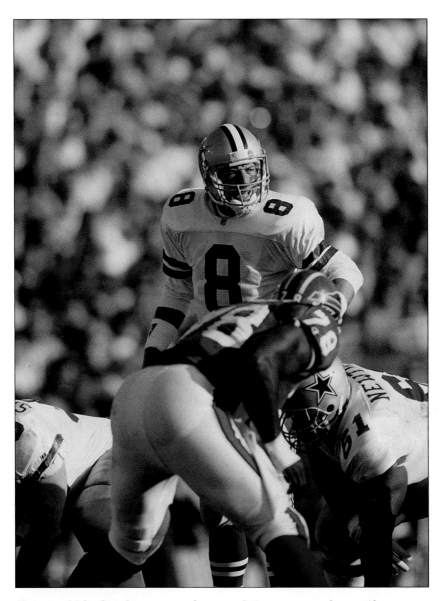

Troy and his Cowboys were in complete command over the Buffalo Bills in Super Bowl XXVII.

---　★　★　★　---

The next season was a mirror of 1992's triumphs. Dallas plowed through its enemies like a runaway train. Engineering that train was Troy Aikman. Again the Cowboys crushed their opposition in the playoffs. Once again, they faced the Buffalo Bills in the Super Bowl. Same two teams, same result. This time Dallas won Super Bowl XXVIII by the score of 30-13. The Cowboys had now recorded two straight NFL championships. It was a rare achievement in modern sports — a champion that repeats. In almost 30 years of Super Bowl history, only four teams have repeated as champions. Dallas was now without question the strongest team in the land. Some football writers argued that these Cowboys were the best team in football history. All this from a club that finished 1-15 and dead last a brief four years before!

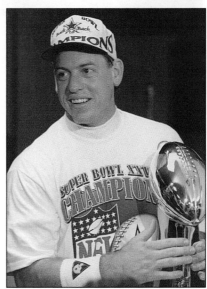

Above: After winning the
1994 Super Bowl, Troy
and coach Jimmy Jones
celebrate in the locker room.
Right: Troy holds the
cherished Super Bowl
trophy for the second
year in a row.

A Super Bowl hero, Troy became an immediate national celebrity; here, he visits Jay Leno on "The Tonight Show."

Success meant fame for the leader of America's Team. Troy regularly spoke at news conferences to dozens of writers in front of TV cameras. He appeared on talk shows such as "Good Morning America" and "The Tonight Show." Viewers saw a muscular, blond-haired young man with movie-star good looks. Talking with a slight southwestern twang, he exhibited a humble, "aw shucks" attitude. He said that football players should not be thought of as heroes. Doctors, teachers, policemen...people in the helping professions were the real American heroes. Troy says that as a kid, he wanted to become a doctor.

Troy is uncomfortable being so famous that people recognize him wherever he goes. "Everyone wants to talk to you," he says. "Everyone wants to touch you. It's exhausting."

But Troy cannot escape his image. He is a handsome bachelor, making him the object of many young women's dreams. He is rich, having signed a $50 million contract in 1993. It was the biggest contract ever given to a pro football player. Still, fame has its drawbacks. He has little privacy. "You know, I wish there was a switch that I could flip, where no one knows me....Unfortunately, that's impossible."

Although he is constantly in the public eye, the media often overlook the good work he does off the field. Troy heads the Troy Aikman Foundation, which gives financial aid to poor children and their families. The foundation awards college scholarships to kids from Henryetta High School, and it helped to build a $250,000 fitness center for the town's use. He works without pay to plan fundraising events for his foundation. Friends say he takes his laptop computer on road trips so he can plan the foundation's budget and help more kids in need.

A defensive lineman dumps Troy on his head — one of the many scary moments in Troy's eventful career.

On the field, there is a dangerous side to Troy's overwhelming desire to win. He will delay a pass until the last critical instant to give his receiver a chance to break free. He will hold onto the ball even when a fierce 300-pound lineman is racing at him full speed. This style of play invites injuries. He was hit on the head and suffered a severe concussion in the 1993 playoffs. He later admitted he barely remembered the second half of that year's Super Bowl. A concussion also forced him to miss several games in 1994.

Pro football is a violent sport. The quarterback position is the focal point for most of the violence. About the possibility of serious injury Troy said, "Am I concerned? Yes, but I can't afford to be scared. I have to go back to pass and focus on my receivers....If you play scared in this game, you are as good as gone."

In 1994-95, the Aikman-led Dallas Cowboys attempted to win their third straight Super Bowl, a feat never accomplished before. They started the year with a new coach, Barry Switzer, who had been Troy's first coach in college. Many fans feared that by changing coaches (from Jimmy Johnson to Switzer), the team's unity would be upset. But Troy believed that even if Switzer had a different style of leadership, it should make no difference to a group of experienced professionals like the Cowboys. Said Aikman, "There's more than one way to coach a football team."

In 1994-95, Troy was reunited with his old Oklahoma Sooners coach, Barry Switzer (left).

Dallas finished the year with a division-leading 12-4 record. Aikman, despite being slowed with injuries, threw 13 touchdown passes. For the second year in a row, Dallas faced the San Francisco 49ers in the NFC Championship Game. The winner would advance to the Super Bowl. But this time, the matchup was a disaster for the defending champs. Turning the ball over through fumbles and interceptions, the Cowboys fell behind 21-0 in the first quarter. They never caught up. When the gun sounded ending the game, Steve Young, the San Francisco quarterback, raced across the field to shake hands with Aikman. Young later said, "I think Aikman is one of the best quarterbacks in the game."

***

On the muddy field in San Francisco, the Cowboys failed to take their place in the history books. Back-to-back championships was a superb accomplishment, but they were denied the chance to go for the "threepeat." Still, each Cowboy knew he was a member of the most powerful team in the NFL. And surely their All-Pro quarterback would continue to terrorize defenses in the years to come.

"The primary fact is, I love to play football," said Aikman. "I love the competition. I love the atmosphere, from the locker room to the games." No doubt that's Troy Aikman talking. Everyone knows he's a competitor.

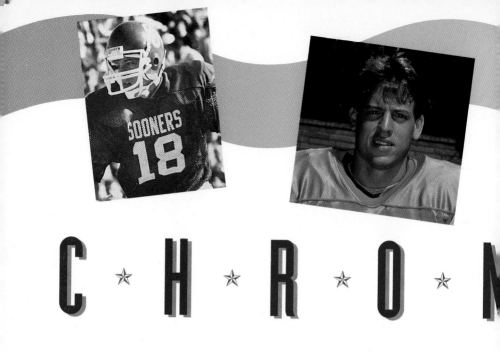

C ★ H ★ R ★ O ★ N

1966 • November 21: Troy Aikman is born in Cerritos, California.

1978 • Troy and his family move to Henryetta, Oklahoma.

1983 • As a high-school senior, Troy is quarterback on the Oklahoma All-State team.

1984 • Troy enters the University of Oklahoma.

1986 • Troy transfers to the University of California at Los Angeles (UCLA).

1988-89 • Troy leads UCLA to victory in the 1989 Cotton Bowl and is named quarterback on *The Sporting News* All-America team.

1989-90 • The Dallas Cowboys make Troy the first pick in the NFL draft; Troy plays in 11 games, but the Cowboys suffer through a dismal 1-15 record.

O · L · O · G · Y

1990-91 • The Cowboys improve to 7-9 and miss the playoffs for the fifth straight year.

1991-92 • The Cowboys break through with an 11-5 record and make the playoffs. Troy plays in his first Pro Bowl.

1992-93 • In his best season as a pro, Troy passes for 3,445 yards and 23 touchdowns. He leads the Cowboys to a 13-3 record. He wins the MVP award in Super Bowl XXVII, in which the Cowboys trounce the Buffalo Bills 52-17.

1993-94 • The Cowboys roll to a 12-4 record. In the Super Bowl, Troy passes for 207 yards, and the Cowboys again defeat Buffalo—this time the score is 30-13.

1994-95 • In another brilliant 12-4 season, injuries force Troy to miss several games. The Cowboys are derailed in their attempt for a third straight Super Bowl. They are defeated by the San Francisco 49ers in the NFC Championship Game.

45

Troy Kenneth Aikman

Date of Birth **November 21, 1966**
Place of Birth **Cerritos, California**
High School **Henryetta (Oklahoma)**
 High School
Height **6-foot-4**
Weight **228 pounds**
College **University of Oklahoma;**
University of California,
Los Angeles (UCLA)
Pro Team **Dallas Cowboys**
Won Super Bowl **1993, 1994**
Named Super Bowl MVP **1993**
Named to NFC Pro Bowl Team
 1991-92, 1992-93, 1993-94,
 1994-95

⋆ PROFESSIONAL CAREER ⋆

Season	Team	Pass Attempts	Pass Completions	Passing Percentage	Passing Yards	Touch-downs
1989-90	Dallas	293	155	52.9	1,749	9
1990-91	Dallas	399	226	56.6	2,579	11
1991-92	Dallas	363	237	65.3	2,754	11
1992-93	Dallas	473	302	63.8	3,445	23
1993-94	Dallas	392	271	*69.1*	3,100	15
1994-95	Dallas	361	233	64.5	2,676	13
Total (6 seasons)		**2,281**	**1,424**	**62.4**	**16,303**	**82**

(*Italics* indicates led NFL)

★ ★ ★

About the Author

R. Conrad Stein lives in Chicago with his wife and their daughter, Janna. He is the author of many books written for young readers.

While growing up in Chicago, Mr. Stein loved baseball, basketball, and football. But he was a terrible player and was generally picked last when the kids chose sides. So he spent endless hours on the sidelines of athletic fields watching more talented players perform. Thus, the author became a sports fan. He is still a fan, and he believes Troy Aikman is one of the best quarterbacks he has ever seen in the many years he has watched pro football.

Mr. Stein has also written biographies of David Robinson and Don Shula in the Childrens Press Sports Stars series.